Groundhog Day

Buddy BOOKS
Holidays

ABDO
Publishing Company

A Buddy Book
by
Julie Murray

VISIT US AT
www.abdopublishing.com

Published by ABDO Publishing Company, PO Box 398166, Minneapolis, Minnesota 55439.

Printed in the United States of America, North Mankato, Minnesota.
092013
012014

 PRINTED ON RECYCLED PAPER

Coordinating Series Editor: Rochelle Baltzer
Editor: Sarah Tieck
Contributing Editors: Megan M. Gunderson, Bridget O'Brien, Marcia Zappa
Graphic Design: Denise Esner
Cover Photograph: *AP Photo*: The News & Observer, Takaaki Iwabu.
Interior Photographs/Illustrations: *AP Photo*: The Canadian Press/Frank Gunn (p. 19), North
      Wind Picture Archives via AP Images (p. 11), Gene J. Puskar (p. 21), Keith Srakocic (p. 5);
      Getty Images: Jeff Swensen (p. 7), Alex Wong (p. 17); *Glow Images*: Riccardo Lombardo
      (p. 9), Jurgen & Christine Sohns/FLPA (p. 22); *Science Source*: Hermann Eisenbeiss (p. 15),
      Mark Garlick (p. 14); *Shutterstock*: Alan Gleichman (p. 7), Martin Lehmann (p. 13).

Library of Congress Cataloging-in-Publication Data

Murray, Julie, 1969-
  Groundhog day / Julie Murray.
      pages cm. -- (Holidays)
  ISBN 978-1-62403-185-4
1. Groundhog Day--Juvenile literature. I. Title.
  GT4995.G76M87 2014
  394.261--dc23
                                    2013026910

Table of Contents

What Is Groundhog Day?

February 2 is known as Groundhog Day in the United States and Canada. On this day, special groundhogs come out of their burrows. Some people believe they predict the weather for the next six weeks.

Special groundhogs predict the weather for waiting crowds on Groundhog Day.

On a sunny day, the groundhog will see its shadow. This means six more weeks of winter weather. If the day is cloudy, the groundhog won't see its shadow. This is a sign of an early spring.

Right or Wrong?

Some people say the groundhog's **prediction** is never wrong. But, weather records show that the groundhog is wrong more than half of the time. Still, it is fun to **celebrate** the day!

Groundhogs can't really predict the weather. But, reporters often talk about the groundhog's prediction!

An Important Time

People have had **celebrations** in February for thousands of years. But long ago, they didn't celebrate Groundhog Day.

In early February, **Celts** honored the upcoming planting season and births of farm animals. **Christians** had a feast called Candlemas. It became known for its lighted candles.

Many Christians still celebrate Candlemas today. In some places, there is a procession and lighting of candles.

During the **Middle Ages**, Europeans believed that badgers and other animals came out of **hibernation** on Candlemas. Sun or clouds on that day would **predict** the coming weather.

German **immigrants** brought this story to the United States. But, they used the groundhog instead of the badger.

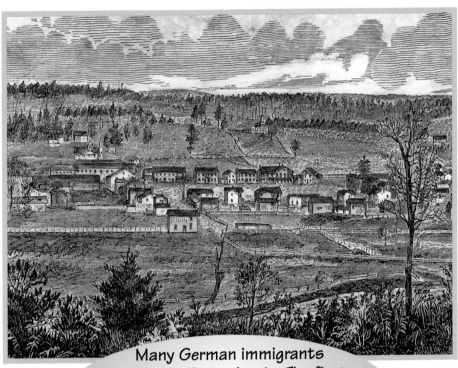

Many German immigrants settled in Pennsylvania. The first known Groundhog Day celebration took place in Punxsutawney (puhngk-suh-TAW-nee).

What Are Groundhogs?

Groundhog is another name for the woodchuck. These rodents have thick brown or gray fur. They usually weigh up to 14 pounds (6 kg) and grow up to 27 inches (69 cm) long. They have bushy tails.

In the wild, groundhogs hibernate from October to late February or March. During this time, the animal's body temperature drops to almost freezing!

Before **hibernating**, groundhogs grow very fat. Then, they curl up in **burrows**. During hibernation, their heart rate can be as low as four beats per minute!

A Special Date

Earth moves around the sun. As it moves, different parts of the planet get different amounts of sunlight. This is what creates the seasons.

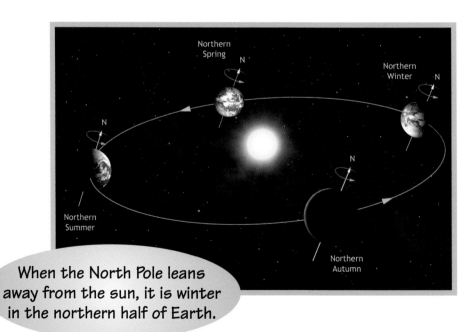

Northern
Spring

Northern
Winter

Northern
Summer

Northern
Autumn

When the North Pole leans away from the sun, it is winter in the northern half of Earth.

Light and temperature cause many trees and plants to change with the seasons.

In Earth's northern half, February 2 is about halfway through winter. In winter, daylight hours are short. On the first day of spring, the amount of daylight and darkness is the same.

Famous Groundhogs

Punxsutawney, Pennsylvania, is home to a famous groundhog. Punxsutawney Phil has been **predicting** the weather since 1887. Some people say there has been only one Phil.

Every year on Groundhog Day, he predicts the weather at Gobbler's Knob. A **celebration** is held afterward.

Punxsutawney Phil weighs about 20 pounds (9 kg) and is 22 inches (56 cm) long.

CANADA

UNITED STATES

New York

●Punxsutawney

Ohio

Pennsylvania

New Jersey

Atlantic Ocean

West Virginia

Delaware

Maryland

N

W—E

S

Another famous groundhog is Wiarton Willie in Canada. Thousands of people visit the town of Wiarton, Ontario, to see him on Groundhog Day. There are three days of events!

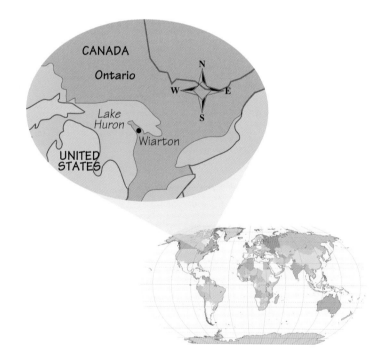

Wiarton Willie is a white groundhog. This coloring is known as albino.

Groundhog Day Today

On Groundhog Day, people gather in places such as Gobbler's Knob. Punxsutawney Phil leaves his **burrow** around 7:20 a.m. People wait to hear whether he sees his shadow.

Many reporters and people watch the event live. Others watch it on television or online. There are parties and activities in town before and after Phil's **prediction**.

A group of men in tuxedos and top hats are an important part of Groundhog Day in Punxsutawney. They are called the Inner Circle. They are members of the town's groundhog club.

Groundhog Facts

- Groundhogs like to eat greens, fruits, and vegetables.

- When a groundhog is scared, it whistles.

- Most groundhogs live four to eight years.

Baby groundhogs are usually ready to live without their mother after a couple months.

Important Words

burrow an animal's underground home.

celebrate to observe a holiday with special events.
These events are known as celebrations.

Celts (KEHLTS) people who lived about 2,000 years
ago in many countries of western Europe.

Christian (KRIHS-chuhn) a person who practices
Christianity, which is a religion that follows the
teachings of Jesus Christ.

hibernate to sleep or rest during the winter months.

immigrant someone who has left his or her home
and settled in a new country.

Middle Ages a time in European history from about
the 400s to the 1400s.

predict to say something is going to happen before
it does.

Web Sites

To learn more about Groundhog Day,

visit ABDO Publishing Company online. Web sites about
Groundhog Day are featured on our Book Links page.
These links are routinely monitored and updated to
provide the most current information available.

www.abdopublishing.com

Index